AN EASY-READ FACT BOOK

Submarines

Robert van Tol

Franklin Watts

London   New York   Toronto   Sydney

©1984 Franklin Watts Ltd

First published in Great Britain
   1984 by
Frankin Watts Ltd
12a Golden Square
London W1

First published in the USA by
Franklin Watts Inc.
387 Park Avenue South
New York
N.Y. 10016

UK ISBN: 0 86313 130 1
US ISBN: 0-531-03774-6
Library of Congress Catalog
   Card Number: 83-51440

Photographs supplied by
Colorific
ECP Armées,
   Ivry-sur-Seine
Dirk Halstead
HMS Dolphin, Hants
MARS Lincs
MOD/RN
Newport News
US Navy

Illustrated by
Robert Burns
Eagle Artists
Christopher Forsey
Hayward Art Group
Michael Roffe

Designed and produced by
David Jefferis

Printed in Great Britain by
   Cambus Litho, East Kilbride

AN
EASY-READ
FACT
BOOK

Submarines

Contents

How a submarine works   4
The first submarines   6
Submarines at war   8
The nuclear submarine   10
The control room   12
The engine room   14
Life aboard   16
Silent patrol   18
Submarine-hunters   20
Exploring the depths   22
Strange subs   24
Trapped!   26
The future   28
Glossary   30
Submarine facts   31
Index   32

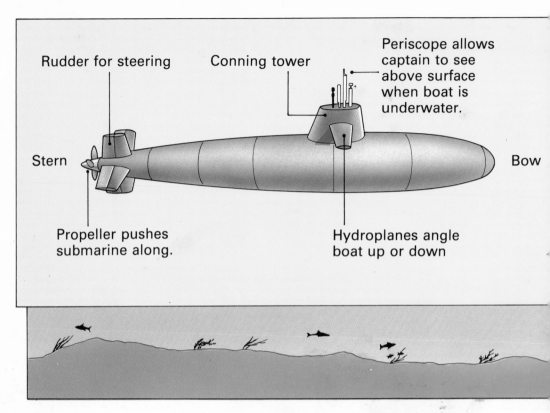

Rudder for steering

Conning tower

Periscope allows captain to see above surface when boat is underwater.

Stern

Bow

Propeller pushes submarine along.

Hydroplanes angle boat up or down

How a submarine works

△ The parts of a submarine. The front is called the bow. The rear is the stern. Poking out of the top is the conning tower. This houses periscopes, radio aerials and other instruments.

A submarine is a boat which can travel underwater. Inside the submarine there are tanks called ballast tanks. They can be filled with either air or water. When they are filled with water, the submarine becomes heavy and sinks

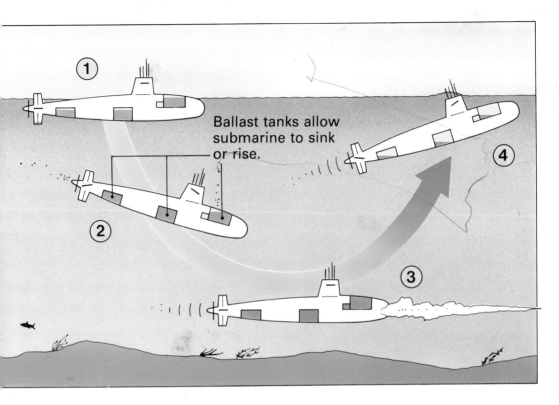

Ballast tanks allow submarine to sink or rise.

beneath the waves. When the ballast tanks are filled with air, the submarine gets lighter, so it rises to the surface.

The submarine is driven by a propeller. There is a rudder for steering. Pairs of fins called hydroplanes are mounted front and rear. They help the boat to tilt up toward the surface or down to the sea bottom.

Most modern submarines are shaped so they can speed through the water.

△This picture shows a dive-and-surface sequence.
1 Ballast tanks begin to fill with water.
2 Submarine sinks, hydroplanes angled bow down.
3 A torpedo is fired and more water is taken into the tanks to balance the weight of the fired torpedo.
4 Tanks are "blown." They fill with air and the sub rises.

5

The first submarines

△ The one-man *Turtle*. It was the first submarine to be used in war. In 1776 it was used to attack a British ship during the American War of Independence.

The aim was to drill a hole in the British ship and attach explosives. The attack failed because the ship had a metal-covered bottom. The drill could not get through it.

The first working submarine was built by a Dutchman, Cornelius van Drebbel. In 1620, he crossed the River Thames in London in the vessel. He submerged to a depth of 12 ft (4 m).

Early submarines were used in the American Civil War. Some were steam powered. The *HL Hunley* was man-powered! Eight men hand-cranked a shaft which was linked to a propeller at the stern. The boat's weapon was a spar-torpedo. This was an explosive, attached to the end of a long spar, or pole at the front of the boat.

The idea was to ram an enemy ship. The explosive would blast a hole in it. Because the *HL Hunley* was at the other end of the pole, it should have been far enough away to avoid damage.

Early submarines like this were not a great success. It was not until powerful engines were used that subs really worked properly.

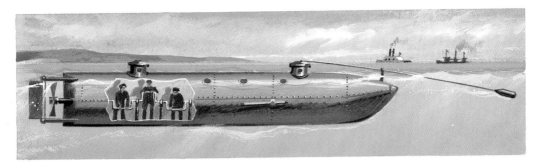

△The *HL Hunley* of 1864. It made five trips and sank every time. It was salvaged after each sinking, but was finally destroyed after it sank the warship *Housatonic*. This was the first ship to be sunk by a submarine. *HL Hunley's* trips cost many lives – 32 men died in the boat.

▽These British ''C''-class subs were first used in 1906. They carried 16 crew and cruised at 11 mph (18 km/h).

Submarines at war

German submarines, called U-boats, fought long battles with ships of Britain and the USA in both World Wars.

U-boats tried to sink ships carrying supplies across the Atlantic Ocean.

Cargo ships were forced to sail in convoys. These were big groups of ships, escorted by heavily armed warships. These would hunt the U-boats and drive them off.

The U-boats worked together in "wolf packs." They tried to confuse the escorts and get through to attack the supply ships. In the end, the convoys, with plenty of escorts and help from aircraft, defeated the U-boats. But the battles were long and deadly.

U-boats sank 2,828 ships during World War II. But 785 U-boats were sunk – nearly three-quarters of all that were built.

▽ This is a German Type VII U-boat. It was the most common submarine of World War II. It carried 14 torpedoes and had a crew of 44. Commanders usually brought their submarines to the surface for an attack. They used the cannon to sink cargo ships. This saved torpedoes. You can see a torpedo coming out of the tube at the bow.

◁ A cargo ship, hit by a U-boat's torpedo. The name U-boat comes from the German "Unterseeboot" – underwater boat.

9

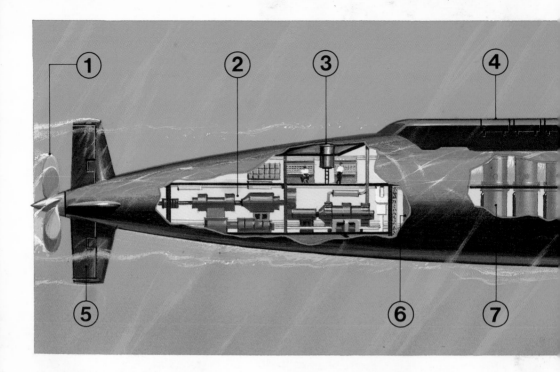

The nuclear submarine

Nuclear power has been the most recent step forward in submarine design. Diesel engines need air as well as fuel to make them work. So a sub with a diesel engine has to surface often. A nuclear reactor needs no air to allow it to work. This means that a nuclear submarine can remain sub-

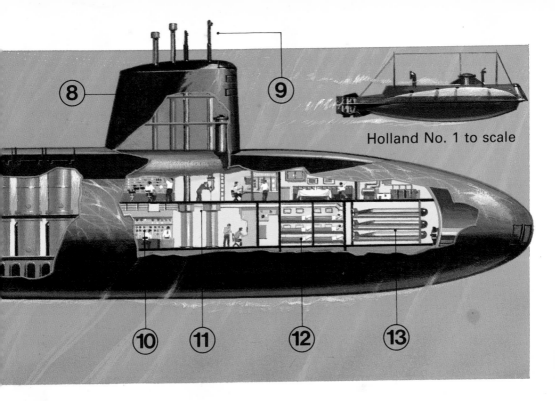

Holland No. 1 to scale

merged for months on end. In fact, these submarines only need to come to the surface to give their crews a rest.

The first nuclear-powered submarine was the *USS Nautilus*. She first sailed in 1955. Three years later, she went on a secret mission. This was to travel under thousands of miles of ice to the North Pole. Nowadays, nuclear submarines often travel under the thick polar ice. They have also traveled round the world, remaining submerged all the way.

△Inside a nuclear submarine.
1 Propeller
2 Engine room
3 Escape hatch
4 Missile tube door
5 Rudder
6 Nuclear reactor
7 Missile tube
8 Conning tower
9 Periscopes
10 Navigation room
11 Control room
12 Living quarters
13 Torpedo room
The small submarine is a Holland No. 1, the first type of submarine used by the Royal Navy.

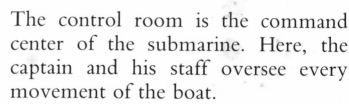

The control room

The control room is the command center of the submarine. Here, the captain and his staff oversee every movement of the boat.

Information from the navigation room, the engine room and other parts of the boat is displayed on TV screens in the control room. These screens form part of the powerful computer system which helps run the submarine.

When the submarine is running just below the surface, the captain can use a periscope to see out. You can see how one works in the picture on the left. Periscopes extend from the top of the conning tower. There may be two or more of them. Search periscopes give a wide view of the sea and sky. The attack periscope gives a close-up view of ships.

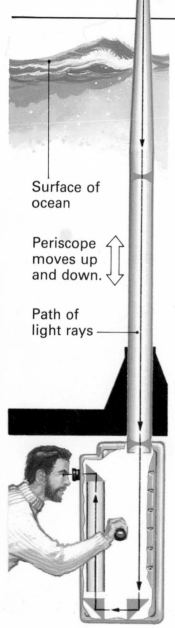

Surface of ocean

Periscope moves up and down.

Path of light rays

◁The periscope is a long tube. It has mirrors inside which reflect the view on the surface. The control room viewer uses the periscope to look above the surface while the sub is below.

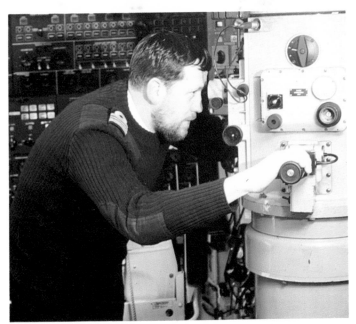

◁Here you see the officer on duty looking through the sights of a periscope. He is in the control room of the Royal Navy's *HMS Splendid*.

▽Helmsmen control rudder and hydroplanes. This is the control room of the French boat, *Le Redoutable*.

The engine room

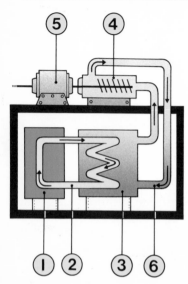

△The reactor and turbines of a nuclear submarine.
1 Reactor contains hot radio-active uranium.
2 Water in pipe boils.
3 Boiling water heats a second water system, boiling more water.
4 Steam turns the propeller-like blades of turbine.
5 Shaft joined to turbine turns the sub's propeller. It also turns an electricity generator. This gives power for electrical equipment.
6 Cooled steam goes back to water tank.

There are several different types of submarine engines. Subs powered by diesel-electric motors are the most common. Diesel engines are used on the surface. Electric motors, powered by batteries, are used underwater. For running at "periscope depth," a snorkel can be used. This is a breathing tube which pokes up out of the water. It lets air in and exhaust waste out.

In a nuclear-powered submarine, the reactor does the same job as the boiler of an old-fashioned steam engine. The middle of the reactor, the "core," is very hot. It heats water to steam. The steam is then used to spin the blades of a steam turbine – like the wind turns a windmill. The turbine turns the propeller and provides all the electrical power used aboard the submarine.

Engine rooms used to be dirty and noisy. Today they are much cleaner and quieter.

◁Engine room crew have their photograph taken aboard this World War II sub. Heat and dirt made smart uniforms a waste of time.

▽This picture shows the engine room of a nuclear submarine. The black triangle is a radiation hazard symbol. Any leak from a reactor can be dangerous. The invisible rays given off by radio-active material can cause sickness or death.

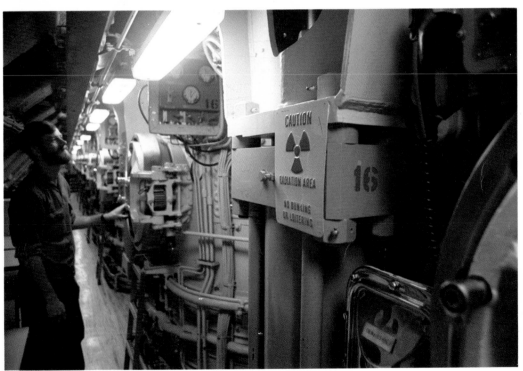

Life aboard

△Here, off-duty sailors relax aboard *HMS Splendid.* They work in shifts of four to six hours at a time.

Voyages often last several months. Missile-carrying submarines usually surface only to change crews and for servicing.

Inside the hull, a submarine is just a lot of metal rooms without windows. They are packed with equipment.

In a submarine, you cannot tell if it is raining or windy. Underwater, there are no waves to rock the boat. You cannot see the sun. The only way to tell if it is night outside is when the sub's lights are dimmed to a soft red glow. They are turned down every night to match the time of sunset above.

Nuclear submarines are big boats, but there is no room for proper sports. An exercise room has weight-training equipment to keep men fit. Chess games and cards are popular and the men can study for exams. The crew can watch films and the cooks make the food as interesting as possible.

Many sailors work on submarines because they get extra pay to make up for the cramped conditions.

△ The kitchen on a boat is called the galley. Here, cooks prepare all the food eaten aboard. Fresh water is no problem. Special machines remove the salt from seawater, making it fresh and good to drink.

Silent patrol

△Aircraft carriers always have an escort group of ships to protect them. This submarine is part of the escort group of the giant carrier *USS John F Kennedy*.

When a submarine carrying missiles leaves port, it heads out on a patrol lasting ten weeks or longer. After diving, the captain reads his "sealed orders" – secret instructions for the patrol. The sub then heads for its target cruising area, deep in the ocean.

During the trip, there are regular housekeeping tasks – cleaning, navigation, equipment checks and many other jobs. The crew wear radiation

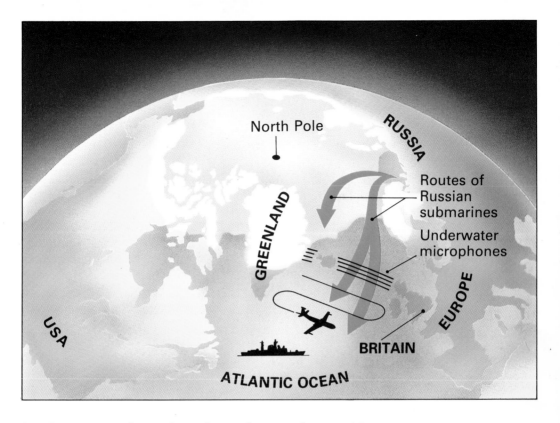

North Pole

RUSSIA

Routes of
Russian
submarines

Underwater
microphones

GREENLAND

EUROPE

USA

BRITAIN

ATLANTIC OCEAN

badges on their lapels. These show if anyone has received an accidental dose of radiation.

A vital job during the patrol is missile-firing practice. The boat is put on full alert. All firing roles are practised, except the launch itself.

In the Atlantic, submarines of Western navies have a special job. They keep track of all Russian subs coming from their bases in the Arctic.

△This map shows the scene for the deadly game of cat-and-mouse which navies play in the Atlantic.

Russian subs have to pass between Greenland and Britain to reach the deeps of the Atlantic Ocean. Here, ships and planes of Western navies keep track of them. Beneath the waves, submarines join in the search.

Submarine-hunters

Submarines usually cruise slowly and quietly to avoid detection. They can be hunted by other countries' subs, ships or aircraft. They all use sonar. This is a device which tracks underwater sounds. There are two types of sonar.

Active sonar sends sound waves out into the sea. Microphones pick up the echoes reflected back by objects.

Passive sonar uses sensitive microphones to listen for underwater sounds, such as the whirring of engines.

The sonar operator is highly skilled. Sounds and echoes may be from whales or fish as well as subs or ships. Only a trained operator can tell which is which.

The sea is full of currents which can twist and bend sounds. Even if a submarine is detected, it may appear to shift its position. It may even seem to disappear altogether.

▷This picture shows ways to track submarines.
1 Plane drops sonar buoys. These are small microphones with a radio. This transmits the sounds underwater back to the plane.
2 Sonar buoy in sea.
3 Helicopter with sonar, dipping it into sea on the end of a cable.
4 Warship with a sonar mounted under its hull.
5 Submarine fires a torpedo at its target, another submarine.

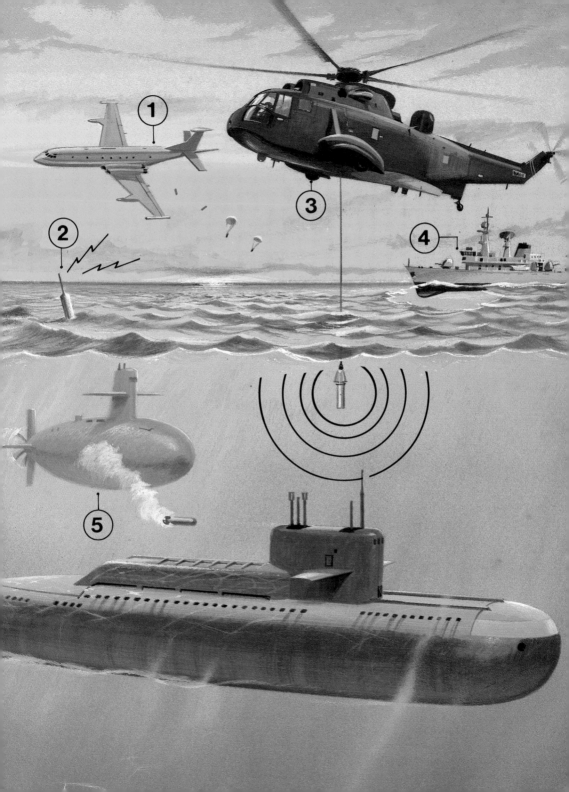

Exploring the depths

Undersea exploration is now very important. Oil and gas companies work to open new wells on seabeds all over the world.

Many underwater craft have been built for these operations. They do not look much like military submarines. Craft like *Aluminaut*, *Deep Quest* and *Deepstar 4,000* look more like robots from science-fiction stories.

Exploring the ocean floors presents a big problem – water pressure. At about 6 miles (10 km) down, water presses down at over 14,223 lb/sq in (1,000 kg/sq cm). This is enough to crush the hull of an ordinary submarine flat as a pancake.

Yet the French *Trieste* has gone deeper than this! The sausage-shaped research craft went down the Challenger Deep in the Pacific Ocean. The *Trieste* reached a depth of 35,810 ft (10,912 m).

▷ This picture shows a variety of underwater exploration craft. Sea creatures are shown at depths at which they are normally found.

1 World War II U-boat
2 Shark
3 *Deepstar 4,000*
4 Whale
5 Angler fish
6 *Deep Quest*
7 Gulper eel
8 *Aluminaut*
9 Squid
10 *Trieste*

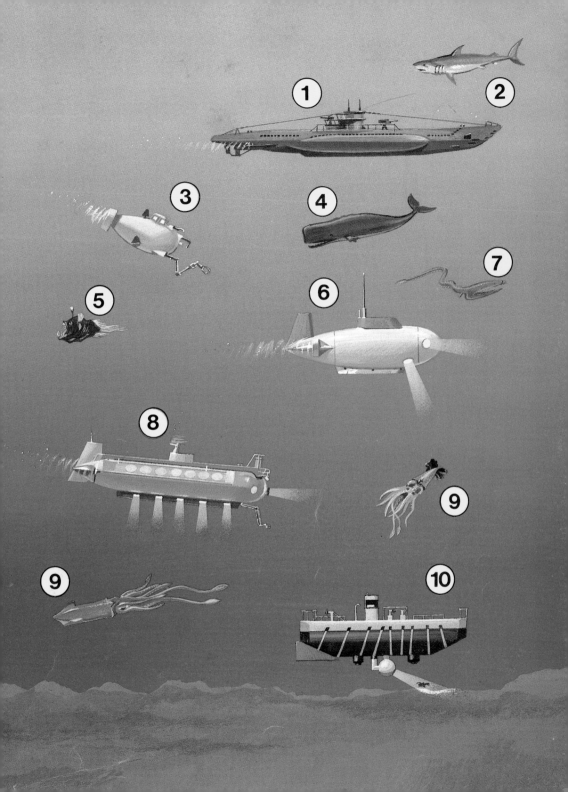

Strange subs

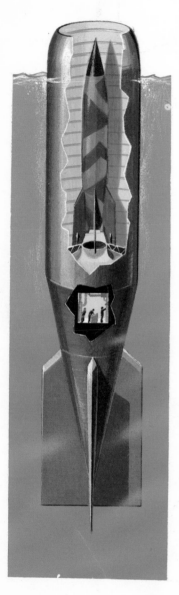

Many strange submarine ideas have been tried out. One not very successful 1920s sub had a huge gun. It fired shells weighing a tonne each. Some World War II submarines flew man-carrying kites into the air. The idea was that the pilot could be a high-flying lookout to spot enemy ships.

Various countries have built midget submarines. These could cruise through the corners and shallows of rivers and harbors. Some even had wheels to crawl along the seabed.

Another idea of World War II was a rocket-carrying sub. The idea was very much like the missile boats of today. You can see a picture of the rocket submarine on the left. A bullet-shaped carrier contained a V-2 missile which would roar off to hit a city hundreds of miles away. The idea was a clever one, but luckily none of the carriers were finished before the war ended.

◁Italian divers took these "human torpedoes" into harbors to try to sink ships moored at anchor.

▽Japanese I–400 subs each carried three planes. The aircraft were carried in a big hangar under the submarine's conning tower. The planes took off from a long catapult.

Trapped!

▽Here you see a rescue being carried out by DSRVs (Deep Submerged Rescue Vehicles). Each DSRV can carry 24 people and can dive to 3,510 ft (1,070 m). DSRVs can be carried in cargo planes to get them quickly to accident areas.

If anything goes wrong in a submarine, the vessel can quickly get into serious trouble. A leak, damaged hydroplanes or a fouled propeller are things that anyone in a submarine fears most. The powerful vessel can suddenly turn into a big metal coffin.

If an emergency does happen, the crew must react quickly and calmly to

save the submarine. If the craft settles on the seabed, the crew can do one of two things. In fairly shallow waters, they can try the emergency escape hatches and swim to the surface. But in deeper waters, a radio buoy must be sent to the surface where it will transmit an emergency signal. Then all the sailors can do is wait.

If they are lucky, rescue craft like the ones shown below will be used. A metal skirt links the rescue submarine to the escape hatch. The men can then escape to safety, 24 at a time.

The future

In the future, people will be mining in deep and dangerous waters – perhaps drilling for oil under the polar ice caps. Projects like these will depend heavily on submarines.

Underwater bulldozers will scrape away unwanted material from the seabed. Robot builders will construct underwater mining headquarters. Oil and other minerals will be loaded aboard giant cargo subs.

Military submarines may become less important. A new type of laser now being developed may be able to spot submarines. The laser's intense blue-green light can pass through sea-water, unlike ordinary light or radio waves. If submarines can be easily detected underwater, there will be no hiding place for them in the ocean depths. Such a laser could be mounted aboard a satellite as a high-flying "sky spy."

▷This picture shows various machines which could be a part of tomorrow's underwater world.
1 Robot mini-sub with walker legs approaches a sea-bed oil-well unit. The long cable carries information to the operating crew on the surface.
2 Oil-well unit monitors flow of oil from undersea oil field.
3 Whale-shaped giant cargo submarine.
4 Aerosub can take off and fly like an aircraft.
5 High in orbit, a satellite uses a blue-green laser which can penetrate the ocean depths.

Glossary

Here is a list of some of the technical words in this book.

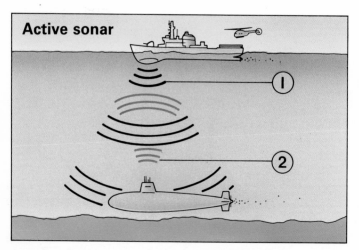

Active sonar

△Ship sends out powerful sound waves (1). Microphones listen out for any echoes (2) reflected back by underwater objects. Passive sonar simply listens for any sounds.

Ballast tank
Tanks used to let a sub rise or sink. They are either filled with water or "blown" with air from high-pressure tanks.

Conning tower
Tower on which periscopes and radio aerials are mounted. When the submarine is on the surface, members of the crew may stand on a platform at the top. Also known as the fin or sail.

Challenger Deep
A steep-sided gorge in the Marianas Trench. The Marianas Trench is the deepest point in the seas. It is in the Pacific Ocean.

Convoy
Group of ships, sailing together for protection.

Hydroplane
Wing-like fin sticking out either side of a submarine at the front and back. Used to angle the bow up or down.

Ice cap
Thick sheets of ice surrounding the north and south poles. Submarines can dive under the north polar ice cap. In the south, the ice rests on the continent of Antarctica.

Laser
Intense beam of light. Blue-green lasers may be able to "see" through the ocean in the future.

Radio-active
Some minerals, such as uranium, give off invisible rays. In anything but the tiniest doses, the rays can be extremely dangerous, leading to all kinds of illness. The crew in nuclear submarines are well protected.

Submarine facts

Here are some interesting facts about the world of submarines.

The fastest submarine
This is a Russian type, the *Alfa* class. These subs can reach underwater speeds of over 48 mph (78 km/h). They have crews of 60.

The largest submarine
This is shown in the picture below. It is a Russian missile-carrying boat of the *Typhoon* class. It weighs over 30,000 tons and is about 558 ft (170 m) long. *Typhoon* submarines each carry 20 missiles, stored in tubes ahead of the conning tower. They have crews of 150.

Subs or boats?
Submariners call a submarine a "boat" not a ship.

Most common submarine
The most common nuclear submarine is the American *Sturgeon* class. There are 37 of them. They are to be replaced by the *Los Angeles* class, of which 55 are planned.

Air for diesels
Early subs mostly had diesel engines which need lots of air, as well as fuel, to work. Running on the surface was fine, but electric motors had to be used underwater.

The invention of the snorkel tube got over this problem. It is a twin tube device which sticks up like a periscope. One tube lets in fresh air to the engines. The other tube gets rid of the dirty exhaust fumes.

Metal hulls
Military submarines normally have two hulls, one inside the other. The inner pressure hull is thick and protects the crew inside.

Research submarines have thick hulls too. That of the *Aluminaut* is 6½ in (190 mm) thick.

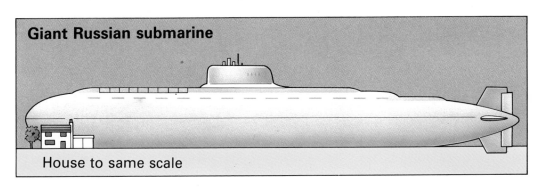

Giant Russian submarine

House to same scale

Index

aerosub 28
Aluminaut 22
American Civil War 6

ballast tanks 4, 5, 30
bow 4

"C"-class subs 7
cargo submarine 29
Challenger Deep 22, 30
conning tower 4, 11, 12, 30
control room 11, 12, 13,
convoys 8

Deep Quest 22
diesel engines 10,14
DSRVs 26, 27

engine room 11, 14, 15
escape hatch 11
exploration craft 22, 23

galley 17

H.L Hunley 6, 7
HMS Splendid 13, 16
Holland No. 1 11
Housatonic 7

Japanese 1–400 subs 25

lasers 28, 30
Le Redoutable 13

Marianas Trench 30

nuclear submarine 10,
11, 14, 17

oil drilling 28

periscope 4, 12
propeller 4, 5, 11

radiation 18, 19
radio aerials 4
radio buoy 27
rescue craft 27
robot mini-sub 28
rudder 4, 5, 11

sonar 20, 21, 30
spar-torpedo 6
steam turbine 14
stern 4
Sturgeon class 31

torpedo 5, 8, 11, 21
Trieste 22
Turtle 6
Typhoon class 31

U-boats 8, 9
USS John F Kennedy 18
USS Nautilus 11

van Drebbel, Cornelius 6